BY
Elfreda Powell

P
PARRAGON

This edition first published by
Parragon Book Service Ltd in 1996

Parragon Book Service Ltd
Unit 13–17 Avonbridge Trading Estate
Atlantic Road, Avonmouth
Bristol BS11 9QD

Produced by Magpie Books,
an imprint of Robinson Publishing

ISBN 0 75251 794 5

A copy of the British Library Cataloguing in Publication
Data is available from the British Library.

Typeset by Whitelaw & Palmer Ltd, Glasgow

CHILD REBEL

Nebraska, in America's Midwest, is a land of extremes: summers of scorching heat, winters of bitter cold, with icicles hanging on the trees. Cattle and crops of maize and wheat cover its vast plains, once roamed by the now dispossessed Cheyenne and Sioux Indians. It was here, in Nebraska's largest city, Omaha, on 3 April 1924, that Marlon Brando (for that is his real name) was born.

He was the third child of Marlon Brando Sr

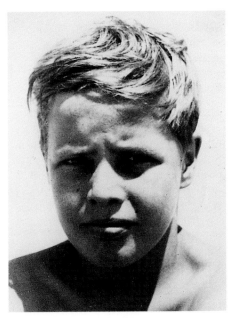

Marlon as a child

and Dorothy Pennebaker Brando, known affectionately as 'Dodie'. Both parents were middle-class and both were alcoholics.

Marlon and his older sisters, Jocelyn (Tiddy) and Frances (Frannie), all inherited their parents' handsome looks, and Marlon, or Bud, as he became known, closely resembled his father. Both parents' families had lived in Nebraska for generations – the Brandos had originally come from Alsace – while Dodie's grandfather had emigrated from Dublin as a pioneering doctor. Dodie's mother, Bessie, had been widowed early in her life, and was very independent. At a time when few women had responsible employment, she had found a job and earned enough to support her family. She was well read, outspoken on social issues, particularly women's rights, and flouted social proprieties by smoking. Bessie's independence of spirit had rubbed off on her daughter, Marlon's mother, which did not help the smooth running of her marriage.

When she was at home, Dodie liked to have the house full of noise and people. She was vibrant, witty and unconventional. She loved singing and playing the piano, and would frequently entertain from her bed. At a time when the sale of liquor was forbidden, Dodie's tipple was gin, poured from a bottle she called her 'change of life medicine'. But her great passion was acting, at which, by all accounts, she was genuinely talented and she spent a great deal of time putting on productions at the local theatre. She played the lead in George Bernard Shaw's *Pygmalion* (no one knows where she acquired her perfect English accent) and in Eugene O'Neil's *Anna Christie*. She was a progressive thinker and very ambitious for her children.

Marlon Brando Sr had his own mineral waste products company, and was often away making sales, wiling away his nights in hotels with a bottle of hooch and one-night stands. When he did come home the Brando household crackled with tension. Brando Sr's moods swung rapidly, so the children never knew where they stood with him. One moment he would be laughing, the next in a thunderous temper. As a boy, Marlon loved and hated him at the same time. His father was both mean with the money spent on his family, and frugal in encouragement and praise for his son. He always gave Marlon the impression that he would never amount to anything and belittled what he did.

When Marlon was six, the family moved to Evanstown, Illinois, where his father was appointed general sales manager of a mineral sales company. His mother still drank too much and was at home even less. Sometimes the children would have to go out looking for her, and bring her home from a saloon somewhat the worse for wear. Not surprisingly, with all the background tension and anger, Marlon showed little interest in school and began to play truant: he vandalised a building, slashed tyres, stole money. And he began to stammer. Marlon was to feel throughout his life that he had a deprived childhood. His sister Frannie, however, described him as 'spoilt'.

When he was eleven, his parents' marriage broke down completely. Marlon's grandmother Bessie took her daughter Dodie and the children away to live in California, and it was here that Marlon visited Paramount Studios for the first time. Dodie had given her great friend, Harriet Fonda's brother Henry, his first part in one of her local productions, and now Henry was making his way in his first pictures.

Two years later, Dodie decided to patch up the marriage, and they returned to Illinois, this time to an old farmhouse with livery stables behind, near Libertyville. Little changed in Marlon's parents' relationship and the couple were soon the centre of local gossip. Compared with many of their neighbours they were extremely well off and didn't fit in. Marlon became withdrawn and self-contained, seeking affection from a collection of animals – bantams, a Great Dane, a Guernsey cow he was alleged to milk twice a day, numerous farm cats and injured birds – rather than from his own family. He befriended neighbours and spent more time in their homes than in his own. He had a desperate desire to be wanted. At school his brooding aloofness, his long eyelashes and sensuous mouth were already making him attractive to girls.

He took a great interest in drama at school and in his mother's own productions. Academically, though, he continued to do badly and enjoyed fooling around – one day he even started a fire in the English class. Some began to call him cocky.

In 1941, Marlon's father decided it was time to instil some discipline in him, along with a sense of honour, loyalty and courage. Marlon was sent away to Shattuck Military Academy in Minnesota, where his father had himself trained as a young man. Initially he became interested in football there and joined their second team, but injured his knee and had to have some torn cartilage removed. He came to hate the place. His only consolation was the encouragement he received from Duke Wagner, head of the English department, who persuaded him to join the school's Dramatic Association and take part in one of their plays. In his second year he joined the drill team, known as the Crack Squad and considered one of the best in the country. Other amusements included farting contests in chapel. But Marlon wasn't to finish the course. Caught smoking in the dormitory, he was expelled.

He found a temporary job digging trenches for a pipeline. But when his call-up papers came, his bad knee prevented him from being drafted (he was classified as 4–F). However, his mind was now made up: his sisters were already in New York, Frannie was studying art and Tiddy, who was engaged to an actor, was at drama school. Whatever ideas his father might have about him learning a trade, there was only one thing he wanted to do: go to New York and learn to act.

FINDING A VOICE

After the strictures of Military Academy life, New York had an exhilarating freedom. Marlon arrived there in May 1943 and moved in with his sister Frannie, who had a flat in Greenwich Village, New York's bohemian district. It was not long before he lost his virginity to Frannie's neighbour, a much older Colombian woman, Estrelita Ross Maria Consuelo Cruz, whose husband happened to be away in the Marines.

Marlon's father had agreed to pay for his acting course, although he did get occasional work to help subsidise his studies: as a lift operator in a department store, a waiter, and a sandwich man. Compared with many of his fellow students he was well off, and could spend time savouring New York's night life, cafés, jazz cubs, all-night parties and the pleasure of getting drunk.

In his autobiography, Brando recounts an interesting meeting one afternoon in a cafeteria with two men. One spoke with a heavy Texan accent, although it was very obvious he was New York Jewish. He told Marlon he'd adopted the accent as a protective cover in the army, as Jews were given such a hard time there. The man introduced himself as Norman Mailer and his companion was the black writer James Baldwin – both at that time

11

Young film star

unpublished. Brando and Baldwin became good friends, and in the sixties Baldwin would encourage him to join the Civil Rights movement.

But Brando's purpose in coming to New York was to learn acting. He enrolled at Erwin Piscator's Dramatic Workshop at the New School for Social Research, an educational centre run by some of the most interesting Jewish intellectuals who had fled Nazi Germany. Some of its famous pupils would be Walter Matthau, Ben Gazzara, Shelley Winters, and Harry Belafonte who would be another big influence in Brando's life. Tennessee Williams also had a playwriting workshop at the school.

Piscator had been a prominent theatre director in Germany before he emigrated to the States two years before Hitler's rise to power, but, for Brando, the most influential teacher at the school was Stella Adler. She had studied at the Moscow Art Theatre under Constantin Stanislavsky, the first person to produce Chekhov's plays. Stanislavsky's innovative technique, which became known as the Stanislavsky Method, or 'Method Acting', depended on the actor actually experiencing the emotions of the character being played.

Brando claims that Stella Adler, who carried on Stanislavsky's legacy, can be credited with influencing almost all present-day cinema, so extraordinary was the effect of her brilliant teaching. Before her influence, acting had been stagey and artificial. At the school, she did not work on plays, but on improvisations and exercises, to focus on the student actors' own desires, fears and inhibitions: she taught them to study external clues to character, and to be natural and not overact. She found Brando an extremely gifted student for whom all she had to do was point the way: he did the rest. 'I opened up possibilities of thinking, feeling, experience and I opened the doors. He walked through,' she said. It was Stella Adler, and not Lee Strasberg, as later claimed, who was Brando's inspiration and who taught him to trust his own intuition.

Fellow students were rather astonished by Brando who, socially, seemed like an unruly puppy, yet when he acted, his performances were riveting. One of his star turns was a very convincing performance as a cash register.

Stella Adler invited Brando into her home, and here he was able to experience a real feeling of family, spending many evenings with

Stella, her husband, mother and daughters, listening to music, talking and relaxing. She became a sort of surrogate mother, not only teaching him to act, but to read literature: writers like Dostoevsky and Tolstoy – and philosophy and Freud. She taught him to appreciate good music and introduced him to a great range of her friends, including Leonard Bernstein and the composer Aaron Copland, as well as artists and intellectuals. Brando's attachment to Stella caused friction at the school, for she and Piscator had different theories about acting – he favouring a grander scale – and they often crossed swords. This in turn caused problems between Piscator and Brando, who would rebel against Piscator's instructions. But animosity about acting theory was not Piscator's reason for dismissing Brando at the end of only a year; rather Brando's overt promiscuity with girls.

Brando had become great friends with two young men: Darren Dublin, a small, bespectacled ex-student of the school, and a fellow pupil Carlo Fiore, son of a Sicilian immigrant. Much of their spare time was taken up with comparing notes on how to seduce girls (Marlon had even offered Carlo to his mother Dodie, who had now split up from her husband and come to live in New York with all her family in a large, disorganised apartment, always full of people and activity). Marlon was an immensely successful seducer, partly due to the technique he had evolved: he would ask a girl out, wine and dine her, take her politely home, then not contact her for three weeks while he dated other girls, by which time the poor girl would be distraught and ready to throw herself at him. One girl he did not succeed with was the actress Elaine Stritch, whose virtues were safeguarded by the nuns of the convent where she was staying while she attended the school). However, he did succeed with a certain Blossom Plumb, who was playing Eve in the school's summer production. Piscator, who also had his eye on this blue-eyed blonde, caught them *in flagrante delicto* and Marlon was expelled on the spot.

However, by then, nothing could have been more opportune, for Marlon had been talent-spotted by one of New York's leading theatrical agents, Maynard Morris, in the school's production of *Hannele's Way to Heaven*. Being expelled left him free to take a part on Broadway.

FINDING A ROLE

Almost immediately after being expelled from
the school, Brando was offered an audition for
a small part in a bland Broadway production, *I
Remember Mama*, by Rodgers and Hammer-
stein and with a star-studded cast. He was to
play the part of Nels, a shy Norwegian teenager
who longs to be a doctor. Despite fluffing the
audition, he was taken on, but at early
rehearsals he was mumbling his lines and was
almost dropped. He seemed too casual and self-
absorbed. His problem proved to be Oscar

Homolka, the lead actor, who was upstaging everyone. Brando's naturalistic performance seemed muted by comparison. But Marlene Dietrich recognised his ability: inwardly he was relaxed, and this gave him a magnetic self-assurance. The audience also recognised this, and as time went on he experimented, changing small details in his role.

But, repeating the same lines, night after night, Brando got bored (this would be a recurring theme in his life.) He started playing tricks on the other actors: stuffing a piece of cloth into the stage coffee pot so that, at the vital moment, it wouldn't pour, and hanging on to the doorknob on the other side, so that when it came to leaving the stage the bewildered actress found that the door refused to open.

Brando claims that during this period he was having a sort of mental breakdown. He lost almost a stone in weight and was lonely and depressed. Others have commented on his mood swings (though he wouldn't recognise it, already there were echoes of his father's behaviour), and on the fact that he turned up to the theatre dirty. He also had a succession of female visitors, usually Eurasian (he had falsely claimed in the programme notes that he had been born in India), and he would have sex in the intervals between walk-ons.

Promiscuity would always be a feature in Brando's life. One of his friends once commented to him that sex for him had about as much significance as eating a Mars bar. Just as his father had been addicted to alcohol, Brando became addicted to sex. It was a way of bolstering his ego, and of being in control. But his sexual relationships were shallow – as soon as the girl showed any attachment, he would take fright. He seemed unable to trust anyone and was terrified of being hurt.

Rumour had it that at this time he was indulging in two simultaneous affairs – with Stella Adler's sophisticated 15-year-old daughter Ellen, and with Stella, though Brando denies this: his relationship with Stella was strictly limited to hand-holding and breast-fondling. His friendship with Ellen would, however, last – on and off – for many years.

It was during this period that Marlon became enthralled with Afro-Cuban music. He had already learnt to play the drums, even before he went to Shattuck Military Academy, but now he bought himself a set of conga drums and went to classes at Katherine Dunham's school of dance. His drum teacher was a Haitian and the classes took place in the same building as Lee Strasberg's (despite denials, he did attend a few of these too). He also took dancing lessons. It was here that he met Clayton Snow, who introduced him to the delights of Provincetown, on Cape Cod.

In the summer of 1945, Provincetown was the haunt of artists, among them exiles from the Nazis: the German Expressionist George Grosz, the Surrealist Max Ernst with his wife Peggy Guggenheim, and an up-and-coming modernist, Jackson Pollock. Tennessee Williams was also there, writing *The Glass Menagerie*. And there was a thriving gay community. That summer, his friend Darren Dublin says, Brando, with his stunning good looks, discovered he was also immensely attractive to gays, and according to Snow, indulged in some further sexual experimentation, though Brando denies that he was ever a true homosexual.

Along with his other affairs, Brando had also been having a relationship with Julie Robinson, a very dark Jewish girl he'd met at Katherine Dunham's and they were both said to be in love. However, on his return to New York, he broke off their relationship.

The war was now over, and after a year with *I Remember Mama*, he withdrew and joined the cast of *Truckline Café* by Maxwell Anderson, about a war veteran returning home to find his wife being unfaithful. He murders her then gives himself up at the café.

Mostly because of its inappropriate timing, the play had awful reviews and closed after little more than a week. But Brando's acting was praised, and for him it was a crucial turning point because of Elia Kazan, the play's tough but intuitive director. He recognised Brando's immense talent and taught him to project his voice. Brando names him as the second most formative influence in his stage career, although their friendship was not to be a smooth one.

Brando's next role was as Marchbanks, the young poet in George Bernard Shaw's *Candida*, a part he took on because he felt Shaw's work would 'stretch him', and indeed he was marvellous when the play opened in Chicago. However, returning to New York, his performances were uneven. Out of work after this, he turned down Noël Coward's *Present Laughter*, castigating Coward with, 'Don't you know that there are people starving in Europe!'

A Flag is Born by Ben Hecht, with music by Kurt Weill, was open political propaganda in favour of the creation of a Jewish state of Israel and, at that time, seen as anti-British, for British warships were patrolling the shores of Palestine to prevent European Jewish refugees from landing. For Brando, this was a cause in which he could feel passionately involved: he played a young cynical Jewish boy, David, who meets two survivors from Treblinka concentration camp in a graveyard and is inspired by a pageant of the greatness of Judaism's past. Witnesses say his acting was extraordinary.

After this he took a part in Jean Cocteau's *The Eagle has Two Heads*, as the young lover of Tallulah Bankhead. By then Tallulah was forty-four to Marlon's twenty-two, and she had a voracious sexual appetite. Brando found himself fending her off not only off stage but

Tallulah Bankhead

on stage too, for she persisted, even in stage kisses, in poking her very active tongue right down his throat. He countered by eating vast quantities of garlic, but even this failed to quell her. Finally, she discovered he was gargling after her performances and had him fired. Tallulah's stagey acting had in any case earned the play a new title: *The Turkey has Two Heads*. 'Next time T. Bankhead goes swimming,' Brando wrote home, 'I hope that whales s★★★ on her.'

To cap everything, on his way back to New York, Brando's wallet was stolen with the whole of his earnings from the play. But a few weeks later, he was to be offered a new role that would change his whole life – in a play called *A Streetcar Named Desire*.

FAME

With his interpretation of the leading role in *A Streetcar Named Desire*, possibly Tennessee Williams' most accomplished play, Brando's reputation was made. At first the producer, Irene Mayer Selznick, had rejected Brando as too young and too 'pretty' for the part of Stanley Kowalski, the crude brother-in-law of a Southern Belle who has lost her estate and comes to her sister for sympathy. But once Williams had met Brando, he saw how powerfully he could reinterpret this originally

Marlon and Vivien Leigh, *A Streetcar Named Desire*

middle-aged character to reflect the brutality and callousness of youth. Williams was attracted by Brando's 'great physical appeal and sensuality'.

Elia Kazan was once again directing the play, and during the rehearsals, along with others, formed the Actors Studio, an exciting workshop in which directors, playwrights and actors could exchange ideas and were encouraged to stretch themselves. Brando joined in.

In *Streetcar*, Brando played his coarse, inarticulate, violent role with tremendous realism. He had explained how he would reach into his own assortment of emotions and experiences, selecting the ones that were appropriate for the part. He would get into Kowalski's 'state of mind' by thinking about the things that made him (Brando) angry and aggressive. He would exercise beforehand and appear on stage covered in sweat. He also had his hair dyed black. His performances were so naturalistic that many people thought Brando was playing himself, although the character was the reverse of his own. It demanded a supreme effort, eight times a week, to appear spontaneous and fresh every time. It drained him emotionally.

Between walk-ons, Brando took to sparring with anyone around and willing, but one night picked on a hefty stagehand, whose punch split the bridge of his nose. Temporarily stunned, Brando lit a cigarette, only to see the smoke rising out of his forehead. With blood dripping everywhere, he went back on stage. The audience apparently thought it was all part of his act, and he managed to finish the performance before he was rushed to hospital.

On the first night, the New York audience had applauded for a full half-hour. Brando was earning $550 a week. He was famous. But it didn't feel real – instead, he felt lost and depressed. His mother Dodie had returned to Marlon Sr in Chicago to patch up their marriage yet again, and he missed her. Brando was living in the rundown Park Savoy Hotel, along with an assortment of friends – old ones such as Wally Cox (from schooldays) and Celia Webb – and new ones like the dancer Sondra Lee. He bought a motor bike and rode round the city by night. And he began the long process of psychoanalysis, which in later life he said he found a cold and unhelpful process. However, he would persist with it for many years, and become dependent on it. He felt an intense need to explore his ambivalent feelings towards his parents.

Some of Brando's friends began to feel ambivalent about his success, even though he helped some of them financially, paying for their heroin (in the case of Carlo Fiore) and an abortion. He moved to an eleventh-floor apartment of his own and threw wild parties, one night staging a mock suicide bid from a parapet outside his window. He was as promiscuous as ever, and couldn't commit himself to any woman. He was not happy.

After two years with *Streetcar*, Brando resigned and took a break in Europe, ostensibly to discuss appearing in *Le Rouge et le Noir* (eventually the part was played by Gérard Philippe). In France he got to know a crowd of people including Roger Vadim and Christian Marquand, who would remain a good friend throughout his life.

Although for a time he resisted the idea of
Hollywood – he felt that going there would
be 'selling out' – Brando eventually agreed to
act in a film called *The Men*, a production by
Stanley Kramer with Fred Zinnemann
directing and with a script by Carl Foreman.
Set in the paraplegic ward of an army veterans'
hospital, Brando played a young army officer,
struggling to come to terms with being para-
lysed from the waist down. To make the role
authentic, he spent time living in a wheelchair
in a real veterans' hospital and was immensely
moved by the experience.

During filming he found it an enormous strain
to be surrounded by equipment: booms,
cameras etc. Nor did he behave like a typical
star, in that he was fairly uncooperative with
the media. The film was badly timed, opening
in July 1950, just after the outbreak of the

Korean war – but Brando had rave reviews. He was 'so vividly real, dynamic and sensitive', the *New York Times* wrote.

For his participation in the film version of *A Streetcar Named Desire*, Brando was able to demand twice the fee he'd been paid for the play. Before filming he underwent plastic surgery to give him his characteristic Roman nose.

This time Vivien Leigh played Blanche, and Brando at first found her mannered and artificial – 'Why are you so f★★★★★★ polite?' he would ask her. Leigh almost cracked under the strain of having to adapt to Method acting, but in the end Brando felt that she was perfect as Blanche – like a wounded butterfly.

The production ran into other problems: it

was the time of the McCarthy witch-hunt and Kazan, who was directing, had once been a communist. Some of the profanities in the script had to be dropped and the plot changed. The Catholic Legion of Decency insisted on the film being cleaned up before it was shown and some 12 cuts to the original were also made.

Streetcar changed Brando's life and film acting for ever: after the film all actors began copying Marlon Brando.

Brando's next role was in *Viva Zapata!*, a film that its producer Darryl Zanuck saw as a 'big Western'. It was again directed by Kazan from a script by John Steinbeck, and Anthony Quinn played Zapata's brother, while Brando took the lead role. On the surface, the character of Zapata, the revolutionary leader of a

Poster for *Viva Zapata!*

peasant revolt, was something of a challenge to play and Brando rose to the occasion: he spent time living in a peasant community in Mexico, learnt how to get truly drunk and even managed to talk to people who had known Zapata. He asked his friend Philip Rhodes to prepare his make-up. He grew a large moustache, wore a wig and used liquid latex to transform the shape of his eyes, while his nostrils were enlarged with plastic tubes. Kazan, with his intuitive sense, advised him wisely on peasant psychology, and a stand-in took his place for the rougher feats on horseback. Since the Mexican government wanted a more left-wing interpretation than either the American government or Kazan would allow, it was filmed in Texas. Rivalry broke out between Quinn and Brando, fuelled by Kazan in order to produce a more realistic fight between the brothers. Kazan was fond of fabricating stories to whip up animosity and sharpen the emotions. It would, however, take Brando and Quinn 15 years before they discovered how Kazan had manipulated them, and could be friends again.

In Mexico Brando was happy. He had brought with him a pet raccoon that Dodie had given him, and he was seriously involved with a Mexican woman called Movita Castenada. She was older and wiser than he and quite unlike any of his previous girl-friends. She was dark and sensual, and though uneducated, she had instinct and intuition and she was strong. She could also beat him at chess. After the film was finished, she would go back with him to New York and later Los Angeles, and they would live together – on and off (mostly off) – for some 15 years.

As Mark Antony in *Julius Caesar*

'AN INABILITY TO LOVE'

Brando soon tired of being stereotyped as a 'blue-jeaned slobbermouth', but when the opportunity arose to play Shakespeare, he was both attracted and scared. The young Paul Scofield was originally to be auditioned for the role of Mark Antony in Joseph Mankiewicz's film of *Julius Caesar* (1953), but Brando was given the part, alongside John Gielgud as Cassius and James Mason as Brutus in a production that used recycled sets from *Quo Vadis*.

Marlon Brando and Elia Kazan

Playing Shakespeare was a revelation, for he discovered that Shakespeare demanded more than Method acting and his usual mumbling delivery: he had to 'play the text. The text is everything.' The role stretched him, and the film received rave reviews in the States. Brando, however, had reservations: playing Mark Antony without more experience was 'asinine', he wrote. Many British cinema-goers might agree.

The anti-communist witch-hunt was still active in the States. Elia Kazan, whom Brando idolised, had long since ceased to be a member of the Communist party. Nevertheless, he was now hauled up before the House of Un-American Activities Committee. To save his skin, he testified against some of his colleagues, who were then blacklisted. Brando, like many people in the arts world, was sickened by this and felt he could no longer work with him.

Brando's next film, *The Wild One* (1953) produced by Stanley Kramer and directed by Laslo Benedek, was based on a real event. Over a 4 July weekend, a small Californian community had been invaded and terrorised by some 3,000 bikers. Brando played the part of Johnny, leader of the motor bike gang.

A pattern that would repeat itself emerged in the making of the film. A jealous relationship developed between his male co-star (this time Lee Marvin) and himself. Marvin felt that too much attention was being paid to Brando. Brando himself was unhappy with the film, which failed to show what motivated the delinquent behaviour it portrayed. He called the film 'a sin'. And there was a furore when it

Motorbike gangster in *The Wild One*

was released. So much so that it was banned in Britain for 15 years. In the States, along with the T-shirts and leather jackets worn in the film, Brando became a symbol of rebellious youth, of alienation. And a young up-and-coming actor would use him as a role model: his name was James Dean.

By now Brando was so famous that he couldn't go anywhere without being recognised. Girls even broke into his apartment. He was spoilt for choice, although the on-off relationship with Movita continued. After *The Wild One* he wanted a break. He spent the summer touring with *Arms and the Man* to help his out-of-work actor friends, but marred the production by not learning his lines and playing silly jokes on stage. Brando then decided that he would work, after all, with Kazan again. *On the Waterfront*, produced by

On the Waterfront

Sam Spiegel for Columbia, was one of
Brando's most important roles. The film
exposed the scandal that the Mafia were
running New York's dockland and that the
longshoremen's union was rife with corrup-
tion. Brando played a tough ex-boxer who
testified against the waterfront *mafiosi*. Per-
mission to film in the docks had first to be
sought from the Mafia – Brando attended a
meeting with Kazan to discuss this and found
them most polite. Filming in sub-zero tem-
peratures, Brando commented it was 'too cold
to overact'. His final 'galvanic' performance
won him the Oscar for Best Actor, and the
film scooped no less than eight Oscars in all.

After this astounding success, Brando was
trapped for a while in a number of mediocre
films, the first being *Desirée* (1954), during
which his mother Dodie died, aged only 55,

and he began yet another on-off affair – with Marilyn Monroe. He also became engaged to a young French girl, Josanne Mariani-Berenger, but later seduced her flatmate, the then unknown Ursula Andress, and furthermore re-embarked on an affair with Rita Moreno. (Reports describe him as very considerate in bed.) Josanne did not last long.

A musical and a comedy, new ventures for him, followed: *Guys and Dolls* (1955) – which he described as the worst thing that ever happened to him – and *Teahouse of the August Moon*.

By agreeing to play in the film version of James Michener's *Sayonara* (1957), Brando began to show his commitment to social issues. Set in postwar occupied Japan, the plot was about a prejudiced US army major who could not quite bring himself to marry the Japanese dancer he had fallen in love with. *Sayonara* would gross over $10 million, of which Brando personally cleared $1 million. In *The Young Lions* of the following year, he fell out with its author, Irwin Shaw, when he wanted to turn the Nazi officer he was playing into a tragic role, and there was again rivalry with his co-star, this time fellow Method actor, Montgomery Clift, whom in fact he much admired.

Then in October 1957, Marlon Brando married. His bride, Anna Kashfi, was a young film star. Brando had remained fairly loyal to her while she was in hospital recovering from tuberculosis and had written to her frequently while he was on location, and his affection and need for her seemed very genuine. Now she was carrying his child. In a telling interview

Brando and Marilyn Monroe at an award ceremony

with Truman Capote – which he later regret-
ted – Brando had confessed to his 'inability to
love anyone': 'I can't trust anyone enough to
give myself to them.' After their honeymoon,
Anna was revealed not to be Indian as she had
led everyone to believe, but the daughter of a
Welsh factory worker. Christian Devi Brando
(named after Christian Marquand, Brando's
handsome French actor friend) was born on 1
May 1958.

But although he was to adore his son, after
only a month of marriage, Brando realised he
had made a mistake. He began seeing Movita
again.

'BEWARE OF COWS, AND WOMEN'

Less than a year after they were married, Anna Kashfi sued Brando for divorce on the grounds of 'grievous mental suffering, distress and injury'. The violent battle for custody of their son Christian, however, would continue for a long time to come.

Several years before, when Brando had begun to earn real money, he had set up a business with his father and bought a thousand head of

45

cattle and a small ranch. Somehow his father had mismanaged the business and much of the livestock had been lost. 'Beware of cows, and women,' he told a friend.

Now, however, he included his father in the formation of his own film production company, Pennebaker Inc., so that, while still acting, he would have a bigger share of the profits and greater freedom to express his own ideas.

Brando's first (and last) film in which he acted under this arrangement – *One-eyed Jacks* – was a Western intended to show Indians in a favourable light. He hated the stereotyped image they usually had in Hollywood productions and vowed never to have an Indian killed in any of his own. He took over *One-eyed*'s direction after falling out with Stanley

Kubrick, but in the end produced only a mediocre film, almost $4 million over budget. More than 200 miles of film had been used, Brando had little experience of editing, and its release was over a year late.

In *The Fugitive Kind* (1960), based on a play by Tennessee Williams and directed by Sidney Lumet, Brando played opposite the sultry Italian actress Anna Magnani, but the two were at odds (Brando claims that the older actress was miffed because he never made a pass, and in the end he had to fight off her advances). The film was a box office flop, though Brando had demanded and obtained a fee of $1 million for his appearance in it.

Brando needed more money to make good his father's losses and pay for his divorce. He agreed to the part of Fletcher Christian in the remake of *Mutiny on the Bounty* (1962). Pitcairn Island, where the sailors had landed in real life, was transposed to as yet unspoilt Tahiti. Initially expense seemed no object: vast quantities of white sand were lorried in to cover the black lava beach, and 5,000 sets of false teeth were issued and collected from the local extras every day.

Brando began to mess about with the script – he wanted a whole episode added about what happened to the sailors after they settled on Pitcairn Island. It had been intended as a purely commercial film, but Brando did his best to give a realistic performance, particularly in the death scene, where he lay on a block of ice so that he shivered with pain, and his face bore a natural look of amazement and surprise at his final confrontation with death. But he over-indulged in temper tantrums,

Brando with Tarita while filming
Mutiny on the Bounty

moodiness, food and above all sex. Everyone involved in the film seemed infected by the lazy rhythms of the island, and many became infected with gonorrhoea. The film ended up $13 million over budget.

During the production, Brando married Movita who was pregnant with their son Sergio (nicknamed Miko), but it was not long before he had fallen in love with his lover in the film, a Tahitian girl, Tarita Tumi Teriipaia, who also became pregnant with his son (Teihotu). In addition, he was concurrently having affairs with three other women, one of them, Rita Moreno, now attempted suicide. But the worst outcome of all was that the film commercialised the idyllic island of Tahiti for ever.

While he was there, Brando became fascinated

with Tahiti's lifestyle and with Teri'aroa, a ring of atolls some 30 miles offshore, encircling a beautiful lagoon, with 1,500 acres of coconut palms, sandy beaches and wonderful bird life. It took him four years to buy this idyllic place, where he was eventually to settle.

After *Mutiny* Brando sold his production company to Universal, but there were strings: part of the deal was an agreement to make five films for them. The sixties mark the lowest point in Brando's film career – many of the films he made in that decade were inferior and ill-matched to his acting skills. The contractual tie to Universal was a constant constraint.

Social issues became increasingly important to Brando at this time, particularly those relating to native Indians, the American treatment of black people, and American arrogance abroad.

His temptation to meddle in a film's message
(always supposing it had one) often caused ill-
feeling and disruption. Among the flops were
The Ugly American (1963), a ponderous political film, *Bedtime Story* (1964), The *Sabateur*
(1965, released as *Morituri* in the States), *The
Chase* (1966) which, it was unkindly said, was
'the worst thing that has happened to the
movies since Lassie played a war veteran with
amnesia', and a Western, *Southwest to Sonora*
(1966, released as *The Appaloosa* in the States)
– hailed as 'another dog', during the filming
of which he competed with Bob Dylan for the
favours of Pat Quinn.

In the mid-sixties Marlon Brando Sr died. He
had eventually remarried and joined Alcoholics Anonymous. Brando records in his
autobiography how he could feel nothing but
uncontrollable anger towards his father. Much

of his psychoanalysis had been spent trying to come to terms with his father's coldness towards him.

Brando's next film was one of his worst ever: *A Countess from Hong Kong* (1966), made in London with the 77-year-old Charlie Chaplin as director and Sophia Loren as Brando's co-star. Brando's Method acting, which requires freedom of space, clashed horribly with Chaplin's meticulously choreographed style – Brando said he felt like an animated puppet. A frost set in between Brando and Loren and he revelled in taunting her. Off the set he went wild with a succession of Asian women, though Movita (now nearly 50) arrived with new baby daughter Rebecca, whom Brando welcomed as his own.

As a favour to his great friend Christian

Marquand, Brando and a host of other celebrities, including Charles Aznavour, Richard Burton, James Coburn and Ringo Starr, agreed to play in what was intended as a money-making sex farce – an adaptation of Terry Southern's novel *Candy* (1968). This, along with a low-budget thriller, *The Night of the Following Day* (1969), the last of his obligations to Universal, was also panned by the critics.

During this period of seemingly unending over-eating and sexual activity, interspersed with visits from Rita Moreno, Tarita and Movita, Movita filed for divorce on the grounds of mental cruelty. She also asked for custody of their two children.

Brando played in only one film of significance during these wilderness years: *Reflections in a Golden Eye* (1967), based on Carson McCuller's powerful novel, and directed by John Huston. With Elizabeth Taylor playing his wife, Brando took the part of an army major struggling with his repressed homosexuality. The role had been intended for Montgomery Clift who had unfortunately died of a heart attack in July 1966, and Brando agreed to it with some reluctance. However, Huston at last gave him freedom to develop his interpretation of the role in a performance much admired by fellow actors.

FINDING A CAUSE

On 4 April 1968 Martin Luther King was murdered. Brando was devastated. Along with his friends, Harry Belafonte and James Baldwin, he had been one of the first white stars to support King's peaceful protest movement, and had been on the march where King had made his stirring 'I have a dream' speech. He now abruptly withdrew his offer to play in a new film – Elia Kazan's *The Arrangement*. Instead, later that year, he accepted a role in what he has always considered his finest film, but which is rarely heard of today: Gillo Pontecorvo's *Queimada* (or *Burn!* in the US). He was attracted by its message: an indictment of slavery, and by the fact that it was a non-Hollywood production.

In *Queimada*, Brando was an English *agent provocateur* sent out to the West Indies to stir up trouble in a Portuguese sugar colony. In order to get into the part, he felt a need to get to know the black revolutionary movement, and an intense meeting took place between Brando, Bobby Seale and Eldridge Cleaver, leaders of the Black Panthers, a militant group which advocated violent means to achieve black liberation. Seale showed him round their fortified headquarters and became something of a friend for a while, though all along Cleaver felt Brando's interest was phoney.

Filming took place in Colombia, in hot, strained conditions, with the location surrounded by real-life bandits who stole their film equipment. Brando and director Pontecorvo clashed, and after contracting a skin allergy and receiving death threats, Brando walked out and returned to Los Angeles, vowing not to come back unless the location was changed. The last parts were shot in Morocco.

During the interlude in LA, Brando developed a sudden interest in the paranormal. He experimented with LSD and found it deeply disturbing. He had also become interested in voodoo, through a Trinidadian call-girl, Giselle Fermine, though this did not prevent a succession of Asian girls from receiving his attentions as well. In the meantime, his marriage to Movita had been annulled after

Brando as Don Corleone in *The Godfather*

the discovery that she and her previous husband had never divorced.

Brando now took time off on Teri'aroa with Tarita and their son. Tarita was undemanding and their relationship, with interruptions, lasts to this day. In 1970, their second child, a daughter, Cheyenne, was born.

Brando had a brief spell in England – near Cambridge – while he took part in Michael Winner's psychological thriller *The Nightcomers*, a prequel to *A Turn of the Screw*, but by then he had already auditioned for a film that would revive his reputation as a great actor. This was Frank Coppola's *The Godfather* (1972), in which he played the elderly *mafioso* Don Corleone, a compound of monster and family man, honour and greed, although Brando had doubts at first that he could play such a big role. He had conscientiously lost 20lbs before filming started (he had told Stephanie Beacham during the filming of *Nightcomers* that he was so fat it was affecting his sex life); now he found that to adopt a shufflng gait, he had to put a 10 lb weight in each shoe. To age his face – he was only in his mid-forties – the skin was stretched and painted with rubber, so that when released it fell back into wrinkles, and he wore a triangular piece of plastic in his mouth to plump out his jowls. The younger actors were in awe of him on set, but this did not stop him from having fun. When they came to film the formal wedding photograph, Brando 'mooned' in front of the 500 extras, which must have impressed the *mafiosi* hanging round the set as unofficial advisers. (Brando was told that they liked the film, because he had played Don Corleone in a dignified way).

The Godfather was a huge box office success, but it earned Brando very little: he was so short of cash during the production that he had had to ask for an advance, and thus scuppered his chances of earning a percentage. The film did, however, earn him an Oscar, which he refused as a protest against treatment of American Indians by the film industry. Brando became embroiled in the more radical elements of the Indians' cause, sheltering fugitives from justice, and unwittingly harbouring their guns, grenades and dynamite in his mobile home. His interest in the Indian cause, like his interest in the Black cause, cooled after a while.

Mostly remembered for its novel use of butter, Bertolucci's *Last Tango in Paris* (1972), in which Brando next starred – with Maria Schneider – was supposedly inspired by Francis

Bacon's painting of a man 'in great despair', and has as much to do with grief and loneliness as it does with obsessional sado-masochism, although Brando admits in his autobiography that he never knew what the film was meant to be about. Bertolucci, however, gave Brando the freedom to experiment, and Brando described *Last Tango* as 'the most thrilling relationship' he'd had with a director. It could be said that in this film Brando played himself. Maria Schneider commented that Brando was now so conscious of his middle-aged spread that he refused to be filmed in the nude, which is why, while she spends much of the film naked, Brando wears a coat.

Filming was interrupted when his son Christian was kidnapped in Mexico (by Anna Kashfi, it transpired). Christian was already having problems with drugs and alcohol

Brando and Maria Schneider, *Last Tango in Paris*

(he reportedly joined Alcoholics Anonymous when he was twelve), and it is thought that his consuming passion for guns was triggered by this episode.

Sandwiched between three highly paid films: an offbeat Western, *Missouri Breaks* (1975), *Superman* (1978), in which he played the small role of Superman's father, and *The Formula* (1979), Brando flew to the stifling heat of the Philippines to play the bizarre figure of Kurtz in Coppola's *Apocalypse Now*, a film which transposes Conrad's *Heart of Darkness* into war-torn Vietnam. Kurtz lives way upriver and is a mysterious figure involved in 'unspeakable rites'. His final hacking to pieces echoes the myth of fertility and renewal arising out of death. Halfway through filming, President Marcos recalled the helicopters he had lent for the film, to fight insurgents, and

Brando agreed to take a cut in his $3.5 million fee to keep the film afloat, which was by then wildly overbudget. Larger than life and shaven-headed, Brando will always be remembered for his powerful presence and that disembodied voice: 'The horror, the horror . . .'.

TRAGEDY

Brando never ducked financial responsibility for any of the children claimed as his own. But in a repetition of his own childhood, what they all lacked was the stable presence of a father. All this was leading inexorably to tragedy.

In the meantime Brando attempted to make Teri'aroa into a home. But making it into a going concern – with a hotel complex of primitive huts, or with a lobster-farming project – was doomed through indecision and an inability to concentrate or stay in one place for any length of time. But he did want Teri'aroa to be a legacy for his children's future.

By the late seventies – Brando was now in his mid-fifties – he acquired two new girlfriends: a very beautiful Japanese girl, Yachiyo Tsubaki, whose father was a Zen master (Zen Buddhism was one of his abiding passions) and Jill Banner, a girl who came from a similar Midwestern background to his own. Jill got on well with Christian, who after being shunted from pillar to post, was now a confused teenager.

In 1981, to everyone's relief, Christian married, but it was not to last. Christian became a cocaine addict. Then two typhoons wrecked Teri'aroa, flattening everything and causing millions of dollars' worth of damage. Worse still, Brando's close friend from schooldays, Wally Cox, died. Then Jill Banner was killed in a road accident. And finally Christian's marriage broke up.

For nine years Brando took no part in films. He was trying to spend time with his children, and had became very interested in meditation. He toyed with the idea of writing and producing a film of his own – this would eventually become *Jericho*, a film about the US government's involvement in the drugs trade in Latin America, but would not get off the ground until much later. Brando withdrew, putting on more and more weight, and Yachiyo was now in residence in his Los Angeles home. For a time he gave Michael Jackson acting lessons, (his son Miko was now Jackson's bodyguard).

At last, in 1988 he agreed to take part in the film adaptation of South African novelist Andre Brink's *A Dry White Season* about the injustices of apartheid. Instead of his usual fee which ran into millions, he did this for nothing. He was now so bad at remembering lines that he was fed them through a tiny, concealed radio transmitter.

Then, after seven years with Yachiyo, Brando fathered another daughter, Ninna Priscilla Brando – the mother was his Guatemalan housemaid, Cristina Ruiz. He bought them a house, and Yachiyo stayed on.

For his next film, *The Freshman*, for which shooting began in 1989, Brando was paid $3.3 million plus 11 per cent of the gross profits. Filming was in Toronto, and Cheyenne, who had never seen her father working in a film, longed to see more of him and asked to visit him on location, but Brando refused. In a fury she drove her brother's Jeep into a ditch, and was badly injured. Seven metal plates had to be fitted into her skull and she also needed plastic surgery.

Jericho, with its anti-drug message, finally got off the ground in 1989, and Christian was given a small part in it.

In the late eighties, it seems that Brando was making a real effort to consolidate his family. In a television interview he described himself as having 'nine' children: Christian; Teihotu and Cheyenne; Miko and Rebecca; Ninna Priscilla; Petra, his secretary's daughter, whom he had adopted; and Maya, the daughter of another old girlfriend Marie Cui. This makes eight – it is not known who the ninth is.

Christopher Columbus: the Discovery

But tragedy was to strike. In May 1990, when Cheyenne (now pregnant), along with her boyfriend Dag Drollet (son of a Tahitian government minister), was staying with him at his Los Angeles home, Brando suggested to Christian that he should take Cheyenne, whom he barely knew, out to dinner. On their return to the house, Christian shot Dag in the head as he lay on the sofa. Although Christian claimed they had fought, there was no evidence of this. On the other hand, Christian was gun-happy: he was paranoid about being kidnapped again and had surrounded himself with guns. Only a few months earlier he had narrowly missed killing his closest friend in a similar way.

Despite Brando giving what some have described as his greatest performance ever in the courtroom, Christian was sentenced to ten

Playing draughts with Johnny Depp. *Don Juan de Marco*

years in prison; since then Cheyenne committed suicide.

Legal costs for Christian's court case obliged Brando in 1991 to take part in *Christopher Columbus: The Discovery*, though the depiction of Columbus as hero, rather than evil coloniser was contrary to everything Brando believed in. And his role as a psychiatrist in Coppola's *Don Juan de Marco*, considering his complete inability to control his own life, seems ironic, as his recent biographer, Peter Manso, has remarked.

In 1995 Brando was making a great effort to keep afloat a small, poorly-funded comedy, *Divine Rapture*, in which he plays an Irish priest. 'Some might think it a mousefight in a dustbin,' he said, 'but to those striving valiantly to bring this production to life, it is not.'

Long ago, Elia Kazan hailed Brando as 'a happily arrogant, free spirit'. He has not changed. Recently he was turned down for a part in Twentieth Century Fox's *Romeo and Juliet* – he wanted his Friar Lawrence to dance in the nude!

FILMOGRAPHY

1951   The Men
1951   A Streetcar Named Desire
1952   Viva Zapata!
1953   Julius Caesar
1953   The Wild One
1954   On the Waterfront
1954   Desirée
1955   Guys and Dolls
1956   Teahouse of the August Moon
1957   Sayonara
1958   The Young Lions

As Napoleon in *Desirée*